101
QUOTES
to
IMPROVE YOUR

TEAM CULTURE & LEADERSHIP

ALLISTAIR McCAW

101 Quotes to Improve your Team Culture & Leadership

First Edition — March 2025

Published by Allistair McCaw

Allistair McCaw
M

ISBN: 979-8-9922758-5-8
Library of Congress Cataloging-in-Publication Data

Library of Congress Case
McCaw, Allistair
101 Quotes to Improve your Team Culture & Leadership
Case Number: 1-14888443529 March 2025

Category: Leadership, Motivation, Teamwork, Mindset

Author: Allistair McCaw

Format & Cover Design: EliJah Sr. & Jahshua Blyden | www.EliTheBookGuy.com

Published in the USA

DISCLAIMER

INTRODUCTION

Team culture and leadership have always been a great passion of mine. Over time, I've learned that leaders appreciate quotes as another tool in motivating and inspiring their people. I hope you enjoy 101 of my favorite quotes on team culture and leadership.

@bechampionminded

Allistair McCaw

TEAM CULTURE

"The true strength of a culture isn't revealed in times of success, but rather in times of adversity and difficulty."

— Allistair McCaw

#1

"Teamwork is the fuel that allows common people to attain uncommon results."

— Andrew Carnegie

#2

"The culture of a company is the sum of the behaviors of all its people."

— Michael Kouly

#3

"You can have all the right strategies in the world; but if you don't have the right culture, you're dead."

— Patrick Whitesell

#4

"Coming together is a beginning. Keeping together is progress. Working together is success."

— Henry Ford

#5

"A great team is where every team member takes accountability for their own actions and behaviors."

— Allistair McCaw

#6

"Collaboration begins with mutual understanding and respect."

— Ron Garan

#7

"Unity is strength. When there is teamwork and collaboration, wonderful things can be achieved."

— Mattie Stepanek

#8

The most dangerous phrase in the language is, "we've always done it this way.'

— Rear Admiral Grace Hopper

#9

"No matter how brilliant your mind or strategy, if you're playing a solo game, you'll always lose out to a team."

— Reid Hoffman

#10

"If you want employees to feel appreciated, you need to celebrate their achievements regularly and publicly."

— Logan Green

#11

"Hire on character first, then competence. You can teach work skills, but you can't change character."

— Allistair McCaw

#12

"Team culture is not bought; it's caught. It's very hard to make people do things. It's easier to inspire them, and that's how you eventually create a buy-in."

— Dallas Eakins

#13

"A team is not a group of people who work together.
A team is a group of people who trust each other."

— Simon Sinek

#14

"We can change culture if we change behavior."

— Dr Aubrey Daniels

#15

"Strength lies in differences, not similarities."

— Stephen R. Covey

#16

"Determine what behaviors and beliefs you value as a company and have everyone live true to them. These behaviors and beliefs should be so essential to your core that you don't even think of it as a culture."

— Brittany Forsyth

#17

"Positive culture comes from being mindful and respecting your co-workers and being empathetic."

— Biz Stone

#18

"In building a great culture, don't look for the best people. Look for the right people. People that align with your vision and values."

— Allistair McCaw

#19

"The way a team plays as a whole determines its success. You may have the greatest bunch of individual stars in the world, but if they don't play together, the club won't be worth a dime."

— Babe Ruth

#20

"A team aligned behind a vision will move mountains. Sell them on your road map and don't compromise – care about the details, the fit and finish."

— Kevin Rose

#21

"The best companies
hire for attitude and
personality.
The attitude can
be great, but
the applicant's
personality must fit
the culture."

— Skip Hyken

#22

"The strength of
the team is each
individual member.
The strength of each
member is the team."

— Phil Jackson

#23

"A great team
consists of people
who place effort and
work-ethic as a
non-negotiable."

— Allistair McCaw

#24

"A big part of our people-first culture is treating people with respect and transparency."

— Arne Sorenson

#25

"If you want to go fast, go alone.
If you want to go far, go together."

— African Proverb

#26

"Culture is about performance and making people feel good about how they contribute to the whole."

— Tracy Streckenbach

#27

"A hallmark of a healthy creative culture is when people feel free to share ideas, opinions, and criticisms. Lack of candor, if unchecked, ultimately leads to dysfunctional environments."

— Ed Catmull

#28

"Culture is the everyday behaviors of your people. It's how they show up when no one is looking."

— Marcus Buckingham

#29

"We are building a culture of accountability, trust and togetherness. Entitlement will not be tolerated."

— Brad Stevens

#30

"A winning culture is where acts of care are shown on a daily basis. Care is what connects people."

— Steve Cooke

#31

"It is amazing what can be accomplished when no one cares who gets the credit."

— John Wooden

#32

"Culture is simply a shared way of doing something with a passion."

— Brian Chesky

#33

"Without question, the biggest culture killers in a team are gossip and negativity."

— Allistair McCaw

#34

"Our secret weapon for building the best cultures is open and honest feedback."

— Gina Lau

#35

"Effective teamwork begins and ends with communication."

— Mike Krzyzewski

#36

"The culture of a workplace – an organization's values, norms and practices – has a huge impact on our happiness and success."

— Adam Grant

#37

"You need to be aware of what others are doing, applaud their efforts, acknowledge their successes, and encourage them in their pursuits. When we all help one another, everybody wins."

— Jim Stovall

#38

"There is no such thing as a 'perfect workplace or culture.' If you enjoy your job 80% of the time, you are in a good place."

— Allistair McCaw

#39

"Culture is about performance, and making people feel good about how they contribute to the whole."

— Tracy Streckenbach

#40

"Talent wins games, but teamwork and intelligence win championships."

— Michael Jordan

#41

"Culture is the foundation upon which all success is built."

— Tony Hsieh

#42

"The easiest way to kill a company culture is by rewarding high performing toxic team members."

— Unknown

#43

"Teamwork is the secret that makes common people achieve uncommon results."

— Ifeanyi Onuoha

#44

"I've learned that the best teams consist of people who are connected, collaborate well, and communicate consistently."

— Allistair McCaw

#45

"Great things in business are never done by one person. They're done by a team of people."

— Steve Jobs

#46

"Individual commitment to a group effort – that is what makes a team work, a company work, a society work, a civilization work."

— Vince Lombardi

#47

"As a leader, you have to keep adapting and changing…not your values, but how you get your message across."

— Mike Krzyzewski

#48

"If you can laugh together, you can work together."

— Robert Orben

#49

"Your people are your culture."

— Allistair McCaw

#50

LEADERSHIP

"When there is no consequence for poor work ethic, and no reward for good work ethic, there is no motivation."

— JD Roberts

#51

"As a leader,
you can never over-
communicate the
vision and standards
enough."

— Allistair McCaw

#52

"Leaders aren't born they are made.
They are made just like anything else, through hard work.
And that's the price we'll have to pay to achieve that goal, or any goal."

— Vince Lombardi

#53

"If your actions inspire others to dream more, learn more, do more, and become more, you are a leader."

— John Quincy Adams

#54

"Leadership is about impact. If you want to have an impact on someone, they first must want to be influenced by you."

— John Calipari

#55

"What I've learned over time is that optimism is a very, very important part of leadership."

— Bob Iger

#56

"A leader needs three beliefs:
A belief in themselves.
A belief in their vision.
A belief in their people."

— Allistair McCaw

#57

"Outstanding leaders go out of their way to boost the self-esteem of their people. If people believe in themselves; it's amazing what they can accomplish."

— Sam Walton

#58

"A sense of humor is part of the art of leadership, of getting along with people, of getting things done."

— Dwight D. Eisenhower

#59

"My responsibility is leadership, and the minute I get negative, that is going to have an influence on my team."

— Don Shula

#60

"The best leaders are the best listeners."

— Allistair McCaw

#61

"Once you bid farewell to high standards and discipline, you say goodbye to success."

— Sir Alex Ferguson

#62

"As a leader, it's not so important what people think when you come in.
It's much more important what people think when you leave."

— Jurgen Klopp

#63

"I don't look at myself as a basketball coach. I look at myself as a leader who happens to coach basketball."

— Mike Krzyzewski

#64

"Great leaders are able to inspire greatness in others."

— Allistair McCaw

#65

"Before we can manage and lead, you must establish trust. And before you can establish trust, you need to establish a personal relationship with your players."

— Joe Maddon

#66

"I strongly believe you cannot be a great leader without having a high level of self-awareness, compassion and humility."

— Allistair McCaw

#67

"A leader must inspire, or his team will expire."

— Orrin Woodward

#68

"Leadership is the capacity to influence others through inspiration, motivated by passion, generated by vision, produced by conviction, ignited by purpose."

— Myles Monroe

#69

"The mediocre teacher tells. The good teacher explains. The superior teacher demonstrates. The great teacher inspires."

— William Arthur Ward

#70

"The leaders we
remember most are
the ones who made
us feel valued, heard
and seen."

— Alistair McCaw

#71

"The most powerful leadership tool you have is your own personal example."

— John Wooden

#72

"The key thing is really aligning everybody, so they all understand where you're going."

— Eytan Lenko

#73

"Leaders and organizations who are not willing to innovate and change eventually become irrelevant."

— Allistair McCaw

#74

"Become the kind of leader that people would follow voluntarily; even if you had no title or position."

— Brian Tracy

#75

"Leadership is about making others better as a result of your presence and making sure that impact lasts in your absence."

— Sheryl Sandberg

#76

"People feel your energy more than they hear your words."

— Allistair McCaw

#77

"When you reward
or promote the
wrong people,
your best people
eventually leave."

— Unknown

#78

"Leadership is about influence. Without influence there is no buy-in. A buy-in involves earning trust and having a connection."

— Allistair McCaw

#79

"Don't be intimidated by what you don't know as that can be your greatest strength to ensure you do things differently from everyone else."

— Sara Blakely

#80

"A great leader has the ability to inspire and motivate his or her people into action."

— Allistair McCaw

#81

"Good leadership
requires you to
surround yourself
with people of
diverse perspectives
who can disagree
with you without fear
of retaliation."

— Doris Kearns Goodwin

#82

"The secret of leadership is simple: Do what you believe in. Paint a picture of the future. Go there. People will follow."

— Seth Godin

#83

"Before you are a leader, success is all about growing yourself. When you become a leader, success is all about growing others."

— Jack Welch

#84

"Great leadership is about having the humility to keep learning, stay curious, and be open to new ideas."

— Allistair McCaw

#85

"Leadership is not about being in charge. It is about taking care of those in your charge."

— Simon Sinek

#86

"As a leader, I have always believed that trust is built from having the tough conversations, even though they're not easy at times.
No one really enjoys them, but they are necessary."

— Casey Stoney

#87

"Identity as a leader
is everything.
It first starts by
knowing yourself
and defining how you
want to lead."

— Allistair McCaw

#88

"In order to grow as leaders, we must be open to new ideas, new ways of doing things and new ways of thinking."

— George Raveling

#89

"As a leader, what matters most is getting the best out of the people you have. It's all about collaboration and putting in the work."

— Claudio Ranieri

#90

"I think today you can't be an effective leader if you're not willing to be open-minded."

— Toto Wolff

#91

"In thriving cultures, you will find leaders who create continuous learning and growth opportunities for their team members."

— Allistair McCaw

#92

"People buy into the leader before they buy into the vision."

— John Maxwell

#93

"In the past, a leader was a boss.
Today's leaders must be partners with their people;
they no longer can lead solely based on positional power."

— Ken Blanchard

#94

"Culture is not just what we say, it's what we repeatedly do."

— Unknown

#95

"No one trusts a leader who only takes credit for the successes and places blame on others when they fail."

— Allistair McCaw

#96

"To be successful,
you need to be brave,
you need to make
decisions,
you need to feel
responsibility."

— Jurgen Klopp

#97

"The key to successful leadership today is influence, not authority."

— Ken Blanchard

#98

"Leaders who don't listen will eventually be surrounded by people who have nothing to say."

— Andy Stanley

#99

"The best leadership advice I have ever received is: Listen more than you talk."

— Howard Schultz

#100

"The best leaders today are the ones who are listening and adapting to the different generations within the workplace."

— Allistair McCaw

#101

SHARE

Your Favorite Quote
on Allistair's Instagram

@bechampionminded

Allistair McCaw

INSPIRED BY

The 101 Quotes in this book have been taken from some of Allistair's best works: